Mel Bay Presents

Arranging for Hammered Dulcimer

by Jeanne Page

1 2 3 4 5 6 7 8 9 0

© 2003 BY MEL BAY PUBLICATIONS, INC., PACIFIC, MO 63069.
ALL RIGHTS RESERVED. INTERNATIONAL COPYRIGHT SECURED. B.M.I. MADE AND PRINTED IN U.S.A.
No part of this publication may be reproduced in whole or in part, or stored in a retrieval system, or transmitted in any form
or by any means, electronic, mechanical, photocopy, recording, or otherwise, without written permission of the publisher.

Visit us on the Web at www.melbay.com — E-mail us at email@melbay.com

TABLE OF CONTENTS

Before You Begin 3

Lesson 1 - Root Position Chords 5
Lesson 2 - More Root Position Chords 9
Lesson 3 - One More Right Flag Root 11
Lesson 4 - Adding Root Position Chords to a Melody Line 13
Lesson 5 - "Flipping" Root Position Chords 19

    Review - Lessons 1-5 24

Lesson 6 - Rolling Chords in a New Song 25
Lesson 7 - First Inversions 29
Lesson 8 - Second Inversions 37

    Review - Lessons 7-8 44

Lesson 9 - A New Tune 45
Lesson 10 - Irish Jigs 51
Lesson 11 - Hornpipes 55
Lesson 12 - Reels 59

    Review - Lessons 10-12 61

Lesson 13 - More Fills 63
Lesson 14 - Counter Melodies 69
Lesson 15 - Using Your Bass Bridge 73
Lesson 16 - Four Note Chords 75
Lesson 17 - Chord Experimentation 81

Lesson 18 - Conclusion: Follow the Rules/
               Break the Rules/ Make New Rules 85

BEFORE YOU BEGIN

You've done it. You've finally purchased this trapezoidal collection of strings. You've figured out where the key of D is and the key of G, and maybe you've even dared to jump over to the bass bridge and find the key of C. You attack your instrument with great enthusiasm and soon you've discovered the melody lines for several tunes. You learn "Golden Slippers" and "Soldier's Joy" and a handful of other standards, but something is still missing. 'There's got to be more I can do', you think to yourself—and you're right.

This book was designed to help you fill those gaps, by illustrating the techniques you will need to create your own hammered dulcimer arrangements.

I am assuming that you have at least a 12-11 hammered dulcimer and that you know the name of the note on each specific course of strings. It is not absolutely necessary for you to read music to benefit from this book, because much of the information is illustrated in reference to your dulcimer. However, in order to play the arranged tunes you will need to be able to read music on the treble staff. Remember that the examples found in each lesson simply illustrate the technique in question. They are not meant to be finished arrangements. Those will come later when you begin to pick and choose techniques that fit a particular song and work them together into a different and interesting whole.

Each lesson presents at least one new idea and builds a foundation for others that follow. I recommend that you learn each lesson thoroughly to avoid confusion later.

Your ability to arrange music successfully will depend, to some degree, on how much you understand about chord structure. Because chord theory can be overwhelming at times, I encourage you to take frequent breaks from these lessons. Give yourself time to thoroughly understand each level before you move on to the next.

Many wonderful teachers of hammered dulcimer have pointed out to their students that each course of strings is located in one of three positions on your dulcimer. You can play strings that fall on a marked course, strings that are one position above a marked course, and strings that are one below a marked course. We will rely on this system often as we move various chord shapes around on your dulcimer.

Before we begin, let me emphasize that I strongly believe that learning should be fun. When you go into overload with information, back off of it for a time, and come back later when you're fresh again, ready to attack it with enthusiasm. I've added plenty of tunes for you to practice on and you should feel free to let your imagination run wild, when searching for just that "right" sound. When you are finished, the arrangement will truly be yours and suited to your own unique tastes. The more you try it, the better you will become at it.

If you're like me, you'll never be able to look at a simple line of music again, without considering all of the possibilities you can attempt to improve upon it! So—let's get started!

ROOT POSITION CHORDS

LESSON 1

Arranging songs on any instrument requires a basic understanding of chords. There is a beautiful logic to the way chords are positioned on the hammered dulcimer. Once you learn these basic shapes the instrument will be less mysterious to you.

When I use the term **chord** I am referring to a grouping of three or more notes. If the grouping has three notes it is referred to as a **triad**. For the next several chapters we will be dealing only with triad chords. The first triad we will learn is called a **root position chord**. Let's take a look at a root position chord on your instrument. Find the three notes highlighted below on your instrument. (Example 1.1)

EXAMPLE 1.1
A "C" chord as played on the dulcimer

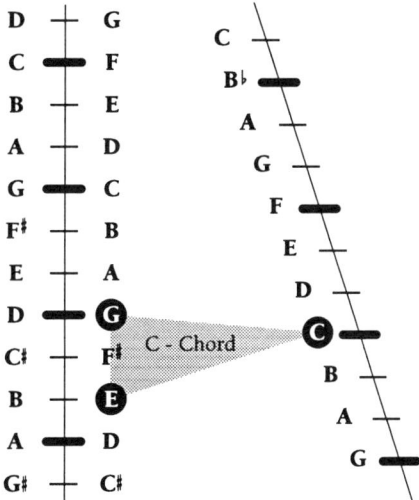

If you strike the "C" first, then the "E", then the "G", you are playing a "C" Chord in root position. Look at the markings on your instrument and memorize the pattern. You <u>begin on a marked course</u> (C) and then move down and to your left to play the note that is one above a marked course (E) and then the marked course directly opposite and to the left of the first note (G). You can see that the three notes form a triangle that points to the right. I call this a **right flag chord**. Play this "C" chord over and over until you can see the shape very clearly. Try speeding up the three notes playing them very quickly in succession so that you get a "rolled" sound.

Look at Example 1.2. This is what the "C" chord in root position looks like on the musical staff.

EXAMPLE 1.2
A "C" chord as written on the musical staff.

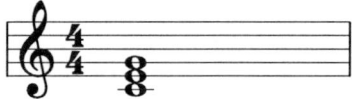

Root position chords are easy to spot because they are a cluster of three evenly spaced notes on the staff. You will notice that the "C" is the bottom note. In root position chords the name of the chord is always on the bottom. On your instrument it is the <u>first</u> note you play. Now let's take this same shape (right flag, root position) and move it to a different spot. Move it to the next marked course up. (See Example 1.3)

EXAMPLE 1.3
F-Chord

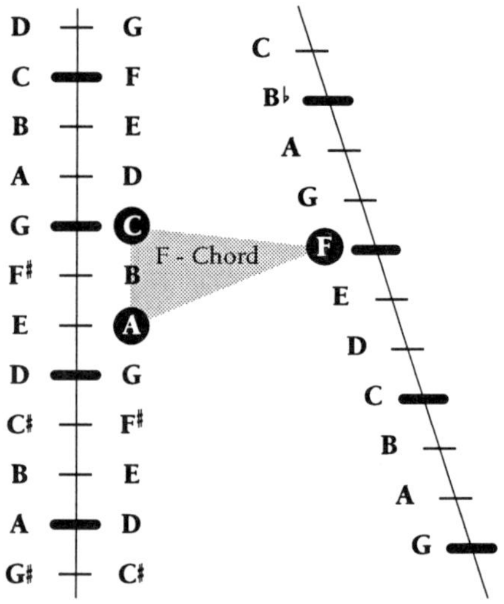

What is the name of this chord? Remember that it is the first note you play, so this is an "F" chord. Play the marked course (F) and then the note that is one above a marked course (A) and then the marked course directly opposite and to the left of the first note (C). You don't need to know that "F", "A", and "C" combined make up an "F" chord. As long as you know this basic shape, and the name of your starting note, you can identify the chord.

You can also move this shape to the treble bridge. It may seem different to you, because the shape is smaller and is positioned over a bridge instead of between two bridges. If you examine it very carefully, though, you will see that it is the exact same shape we have been working with. Start on the "G" and play a "B" then a "D". (See Example 1.4)

EXAMPLE 1.4
G-Chord on the dulcimer

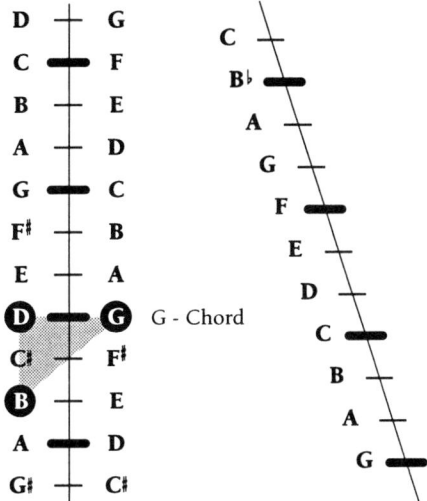

You can now start on any marked course and know the name of the chord. Try the following root position chords as highlighted in Examples 1.5 and 1.6 and be sure that you say the name of the chord to yourself as you play it. If you have a 12-11 dulcimer you can now play a "C" chord, an "F" chord and a "B♭" chord beginning on the bass bridge (Example 1.5), and a "G" chord, a "C" chord and an "F" chord beginning on the right side of the treble bridge (Example 1.6).

EXAMPLE 1.5
Root Position Chords beginning on a marked course.

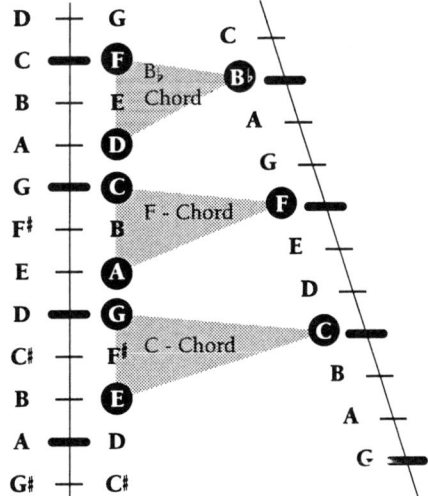

EXAMPLE 1.6
Root Position Chords beginning on a marked course.

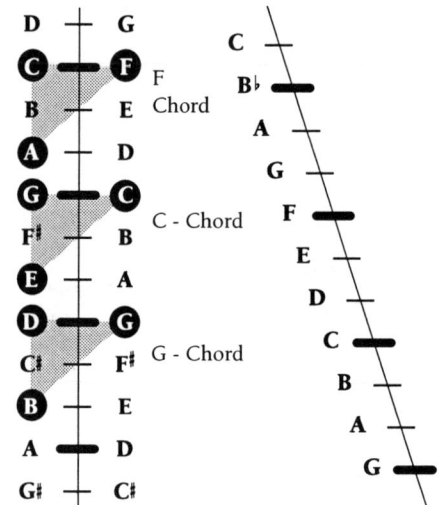

Practice these chords over and over until you can find them quickly and consistently, then continue on to Lesson 2.

More Root Position Chords
LESSON 2

Now we know how to play root position chords that begin on a marked course. Let's take this same principle and apply it to other areas of your dulcimer. Let's start with the notes that are <u>one above a marked course</u>. We'll use the same logic that we used with those chords that start on a marked course. Look at the chord highlighted in Example 2.1 below. Find it on your instrument.

EXAMPLE 2.1

You can see that the pattern is the same one we memorized. We begin on a note that is one above a marked course (D). Next, play the note on the treble bridge that is one below a marked course (F#). Finally, locate the course of strings directly opposite and to the left of the first note you played (A), this note also being one above a marked course. It sounds more confusing than it is. Look at the illustration and study the pattern. It is basically the same shape we played before; we are just moving the whole shape up one course of strings. This is also a **right flag chord**. Practice rolling this chord over and over until it becomes comfortable. Then move the shape to other places on your dulcimer as illustrated in

Examples 2.2 and 2.3. Be sure and say the name of the chord as you play it so that you will begin to make the connection between the name of the chord and the location of the chord. Remember, the name of the chord is the first note you hit.

EXAMPLE 2.2
Root Position Chords - one above a marked course

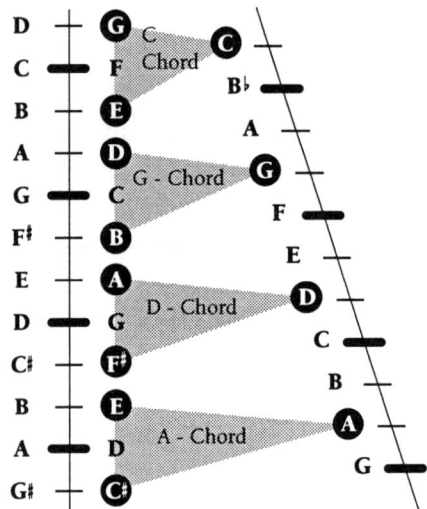

EXAMPLE 2.3
Root Position Chords - one above a marked course

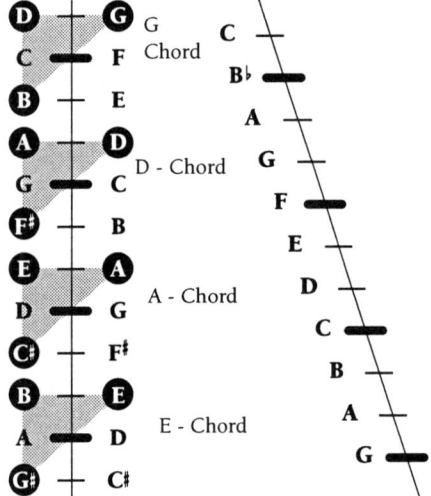

If you have a 12-11 dulcimer you can now play an "A" chord, a "D" chord, a "G" chord and a "C" chord (Example 2.2), beginning on the bass bridge; and an "E" chord, an "A" chord, a "D" chord, and a "G" chord beginning on the right side of the treble bridge (Example 2.3).

Practice these chords over and over until you can find them quickly and consistently and not confuse them with the ones that begin on a marked course.

ONE MORE RIGHT FLAG ROOT

LESSON 3

We have now learned how to play root position chords that begins on a marked course, and root position chords that begin one above a marked course. What happens when we take this same chord shape and shift it up one more time?

Now we are starting in the position that is <u>one below a marked course</u>. We will play the note one below a marked course, then move down and to the left to play the note on the marked course, then finish with the course of strings directly opposite and to the left of the first note we hit, also one below a marked course. See Example 3.1 below.

EXAMPLE 3.1

Once again the name of the chord is the first note we hit. However, when you play the chord you should notice a different sound. Right flag root position chords beginning one below a marked course are always **Minor Chords**. So this chord is not an "E" Chord, but an "E Minor" chord represented in music like this: "Em". Practice the chords illustrated in Example 3.2, being careful to identify them as minor chords when you do.

EXAMPLE 3.2
Root Position Chords - one below a marked course

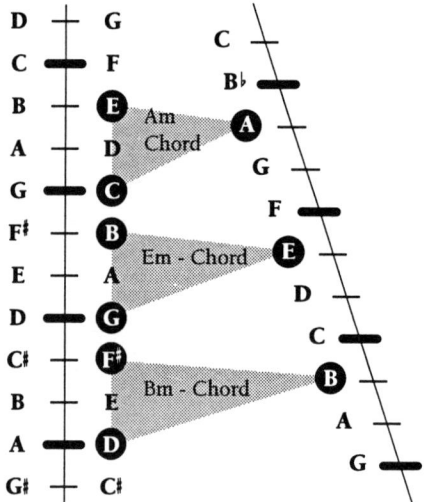

Now practice the same shape on the treble bridge (See Example 3.3).

EXAMPLE 3.3
Root Position Chords - one below a marked course

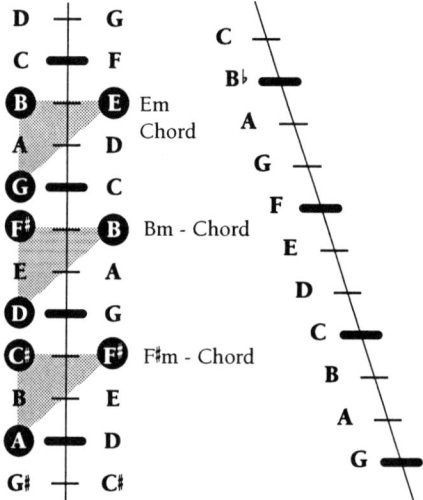

After completing this lesson you will be able to play a "Bm", an "Em", and an "Am" beginning on the bass bridge, and an "F#m", a "Bm", and an "Em" beginning on the right side of the treble bridge. When you are comfortable with the minor chords move on to Lesson 4.

ADDING ROOT POSITION CHORDS TO A MELODY LINE

LESSON 4

Now it is time to take these root position chords and use them to embellish a melody line. We'll start by learning the following simplified version of the tune "Lavender's Blue" (Example 4.1)

EXAMPLE 4.1
Lavenders Blue

Use only the notes in the shaded area of Example 4.2 to play the melody on your dulcimer. We will move outside the box when we add chords, but the basic melody will stay inside the box-shaped "G" scale (not using the duplicate notes found outside the box).

EXAMPLE 4.2

Play the Melody here.

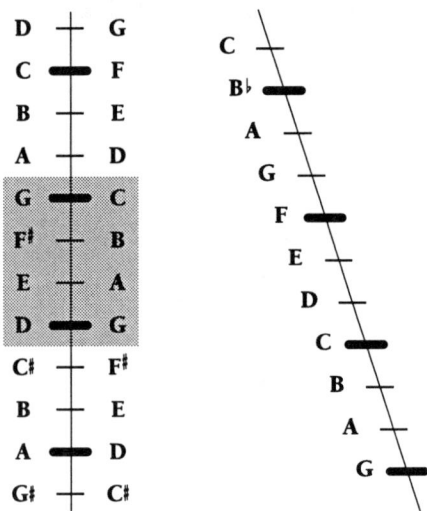

Now we will use our root position chords to embellish the piece. Let's start with the G on the right side of the treble bridge. When we roll a "G" chord in root position, we play the notes in the following order: "G", "B", and "D". The "D" is the last note we hear. (See Example 4.3)

EXAMPLE 4.3

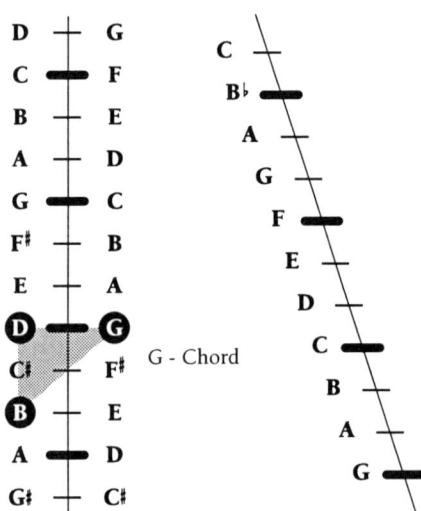

G - Chord

In general we roll chords up to the melody note. The first note of this song is a "D" and we can see from the chord notation above the staff that the chord is a "G", so we can roll a "G" chord on the first note (that note being "D"), and then play the rest of the phrase as it is written. Anywhere that we have a "G" chord to be played and the melody note is a "D", we can add this root position rolled chord. See on the staff in Example 4.4 how we have changed the piece so far.

EXAMPLE 4.4
Lavenders Blue

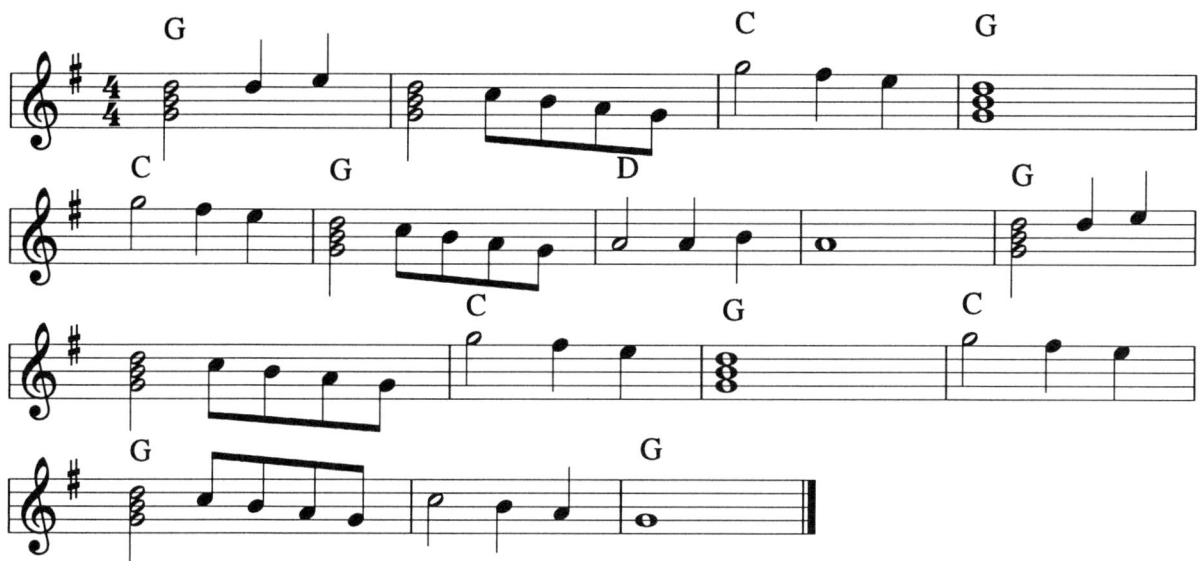

We can do the same thing on measure 3 because the melody note is a "G" and the chord notated above it is a "C". When we roll a "C" chord, the last note we hit is a "G". (See Example 4.5)

EXAMPLE 4.5

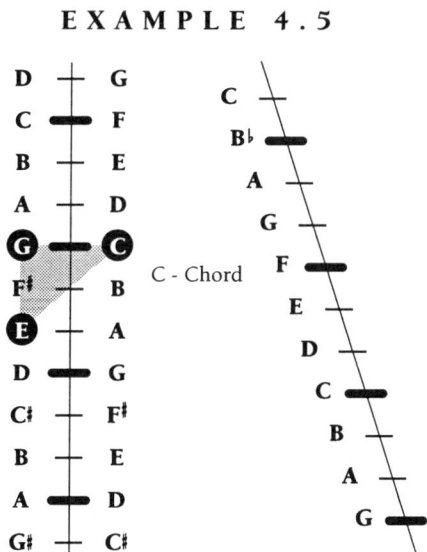

If we add a root position rolled chord "C" chord everywhere that a "C" chord is required and the melody note is a "G", then we have changed the music to the arrangement as shown in Example 4.6.

15

EXAMPLE 4.6
Lavenders Blue

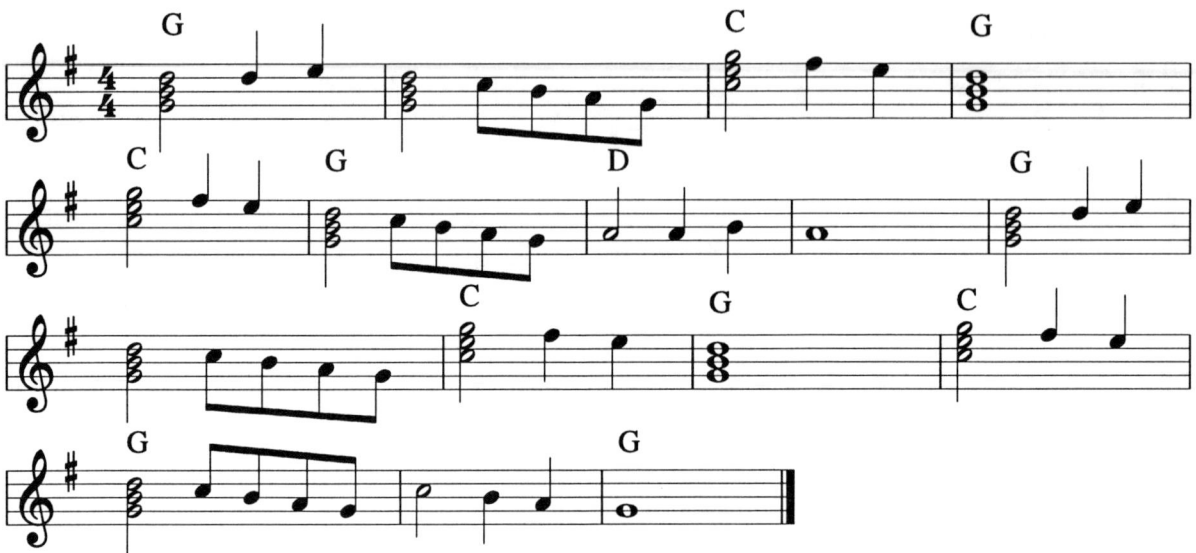

We can continue this logic and use our root position "D" chords to roll up to the melody line where "A" is the melody note. (See Example 4.7)

EXAMPLE 4.7

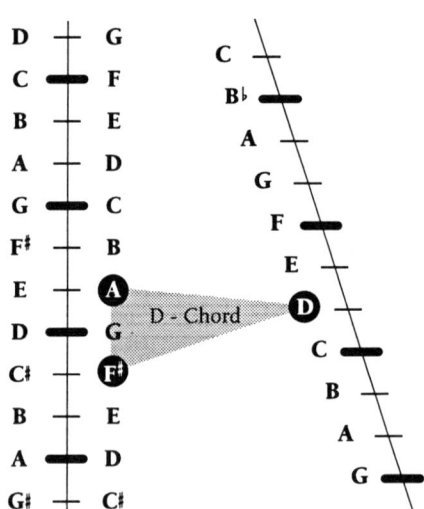

Example 4.8 illustrates how we have modified the tune.

EXAMPLE 4.8
Lavenders Blue

We have done nothing more than add root position chords to fill out the melody line. Practice playing this simple melody with the changes we have made. Think about what hammer patterns make the most sense when playing it.

You will notice that we have added chords on the **downbeat**, or the first beat of each measure. We've left many of the **passing notes** (those receiving less emphasis) alone. This is a common practice when arranging a tune. Try to discern which notes are the most important ones and require some emphasis with a rolled chord. When you first start adding chords to your songs you will probably use them often. Over time, though, you will start to develop your own style and usually find that you want to limit how many you add to a tune. I prefer to add many chords when I am first working a song, then one by one omit the ones that seem to be cluttering up the melody rather than enhancing it. For now, we'll add a variety of chords and then later you can decide to remove some. When you are comfortable with this song, move on to Lesson 5.

ARRANGING FOR HAMMERED DULCIMER

"FLIPPING" ROOT POSITION CHORDS

LESSON 5

So far we have been working with right flag chords. Remember that these are triangles that all point to the right. We can take these chords, though, and "flip" them so that they become left flag chords. Look at Example 5.1.

EXAMPLE 5.1

We've taken our basic "C" chord in root position and rotated it clockwise until the flag is pointing to the left. Is it the same chord? Play it and let your ear be the judge. Compare the notes. It <u>is</u> the exact same chord. By the way, you probably have noticed that when you play a **left flag chord**, you usually need to lead with your left hand. So it gives you the option of beginning a chord on your left hand on those occasions that your hammering pattern requires it. Try these left flag root position chords as shown in Examples 5.2 and 5.3.

EXAMPLE 5.2
Left Flag Chords - marked course

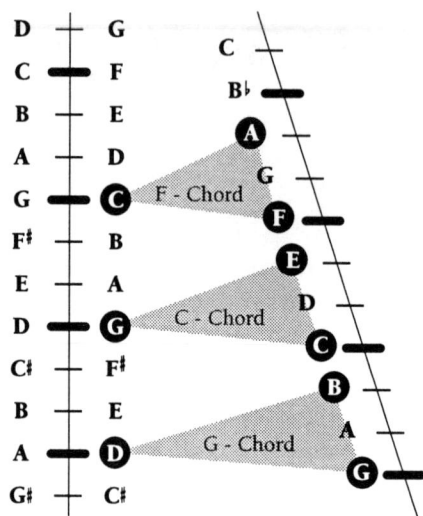

EXAMPLE 5.3
Left Flag Chords - marked course

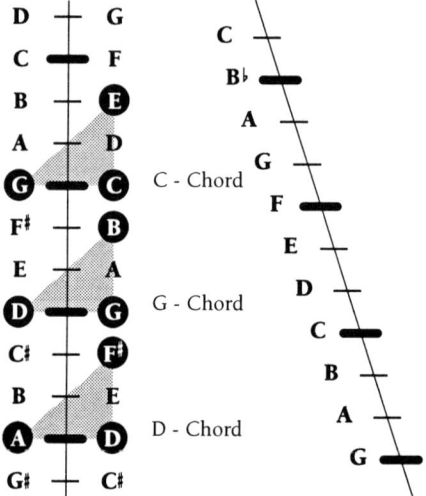

Now let's try flipping the right flag chords that begin one above a marked course. Rotate the chord clockwise until it is pointing left instead of right (Example 5.4).

EXAMPLE 5.4
This chord changes.

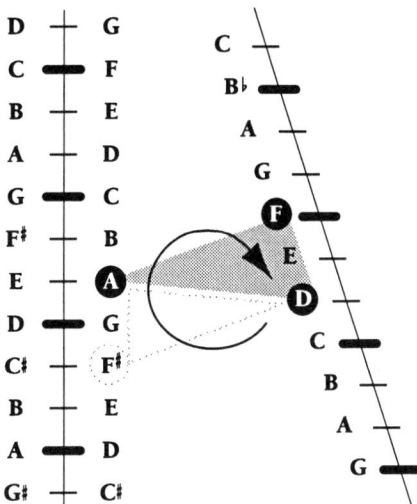

Is it the same chord? What does your ear tell you? This one is <u>not</u> the same chord. It has <u>changed to a minor chord</u>.

Play the right flag chord, and then the left flag chord. Do you notice the difference? The first chord (right flag) is a major chord. The second chord (left flag) is a minor chord. We've changed the middle note from an F# to an F natural.

Try playing all of the minor chords in Examples 5.5 & 5.6.

EXAMPLE 5.5
Left Flag Chords - one above a marked course

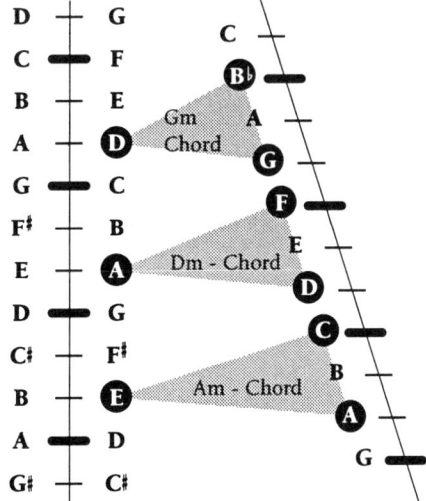

21

EXAMPLE 5.6
Left Flag Chords - one above a marked course

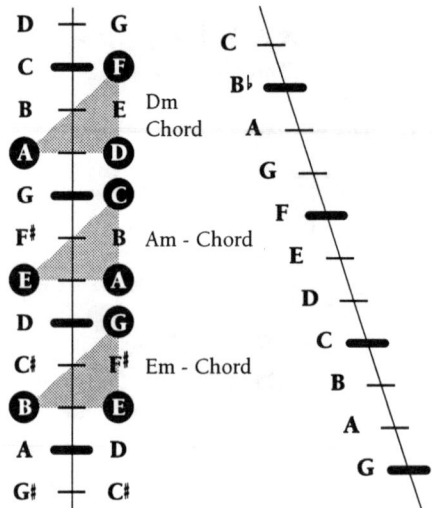

We have one more position to experiment with. Right flag root position chords that begin one below a marked course are minor chords already. What happens when we flip these chords (Examples 5.7 & 5.8)?

EXAMPLE 5.7
Left Flag Chords - one below a marked course

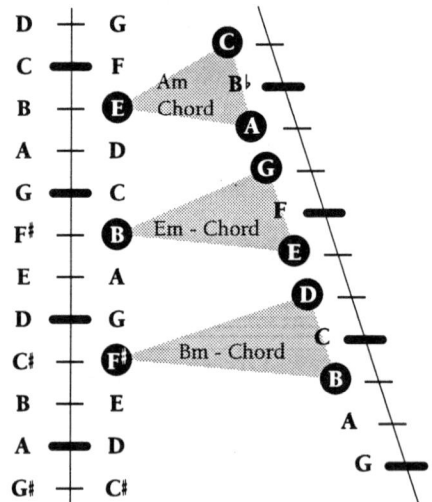

EXAMPLE 5.8
Left Flag Chords - one below a marked course

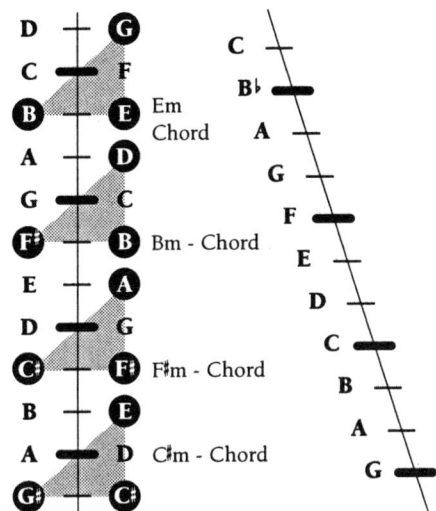

These chords <u>do</u> stay the same. The left flag chord is also a minor chord.

So, the basic rules in flipping these right flag root position chords to left flags are:

1. Right flag chords beginning on a marked course are major chords. They <u>stay</u> major chords when they are flipped to left flag chords.

2. Right flag chords beginning one above a marked course are major chords. They <u>change</u> to minor chords when they are flipped to left flag chords.

3. Right flag chords beginning one below a marked course are minor chords. They <u>stay</u> minor chords when they are flipped to left flag chords.

REVIEW: LESSONS 1-5

1. We can now start on any note on the bass bridge and play a root position chord.

2. We can start on any note on the right side of the treble bridge and play a root position chord.

3. For **right flag chords**, we know that:
   a. If we start on a <u>marked course</u>, the chord is a <u>major</u> chord.
   b. If we start one <u>above a marked course</u>, the chord is a <u>major</u> chord.
   c. If we start one <u>below a marked course</u>, the chord is a <u>minor</u> chord.

4. For **left flag chords**, we know that:
   a. If we start on a <u>marked course</u>, the chord is a <u>major</u> chord.
   b. If we start one <u>above a marked course</u>, the chord is a <u>minor</u> chord.
   c. If we start one <u>below a marked course</u>, the chord is a <u>minor</u> chord.

4. We know how to roll a root position chord up to the melody line.

5. Congratulations! You've learned a lot already. Let's move on!

Rolling Chords in a New Song

LESSON 6

You've already learned much about the logic of chord layout on your instrument. You are also probably anxious to try your hand at rolling chords in other songs that you know. Unfortunately, very few songs use only root position chords and there is still much for you to learn about other chord options.

Also, if you are not thoroughly comfortable with lessons 1-5, you may start to confuse one shape with another, so please, if there is any doubt, do take time to review the information already covered.

I have found, with my students, that it is often a good idea to take a break at this point and give the lessons learned about root position chords time to "sink in." At the same time, they are usually excited to try out this new technique of rolling chords up to the melody line. For this reason, I provide them with a new song to work on, and I give them the chords they will need to accomplish the song. In Example 6.1 you will find a simple, little tune that I wrote that makes use of root position chords in the melody line. Try the melody by itself. (Example 6.1)

EXAMPLE 6.1
The Root Waltz

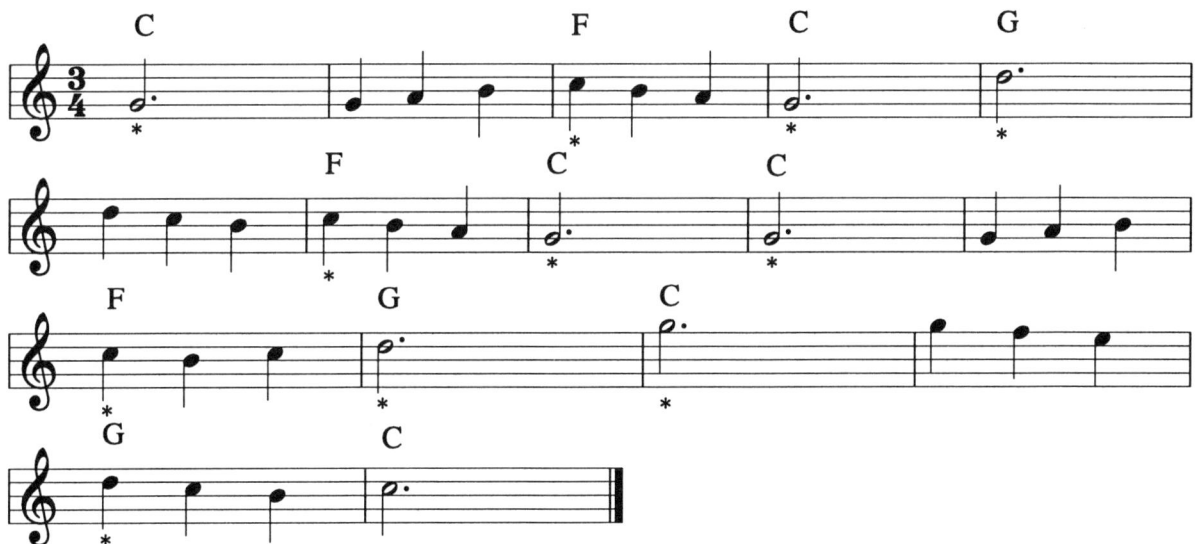

Now try finding root position chords that roll up to the melody line in the places that I have indicated (*). The name of the chord is above the staff. Your job is to find the root position chord that rolls up to that particular note.

Did you find them? In measures 1, 4, 8, and 9 you will need chord #1 illustrated in Example 6.2—a "C" root position chord beginning on middle "C." In measures 3, 7, and 11 you will need chord #2 in Example 6.2—an "F" root position. In measures 5, 12, and 15 you will need chord #3 in Example 6.2—a "G" root position, and in measure 13 you will need a chord #4—a "C" root position beginning on the "C" note one above middle "C." Practice these four chords before you try rolling them in the context of the song.

EXAMPLE 6.2

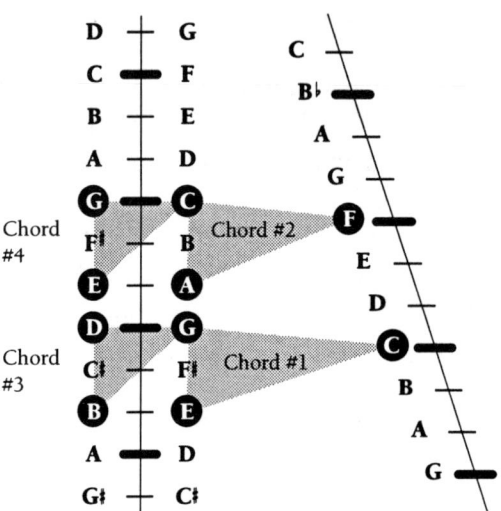

Now try playing the song as it is written in Example 6.3.

EXAMPLE 6.3
The Root Waltz

Take time to practice each step: melody line without any chords, chords only, and then the new melody line with the rolled chords added. After you complete lessons 7 and 8 you will have enough chord theory to try adding chords to your own tunes. Those lessons, however, are very intense as far as the amount of information contained in them. So take this little break, work this song, and see the process in action. Then begin lesson 7 and continue on your way to building your own arrangements.*

---

*If you find that you want to start at arranging right away before mastering chord theory, I do have another book, *Hammered Dulcimer Chords*, available as a reference guide. You can look up the chords in that book and start arranging immediately. It won't explain the logic of the chords, but at least you would have immediate access to them. For those who want to take the process a bit more slowly, just keep steady progress through the remainder of this book!

First Inversions

LESSON 7

In the first song that we worked with, "Lavender's Blue", we needed a "C" chord to roll up to the melody note, which happened to be a "G". We were fortunate that a root position chord, when rolled, happens to end on a "G". But what if the melody note we are rolling to is a "C"? Look at the staff in Example 7.1.

EXAMPLE 7.1

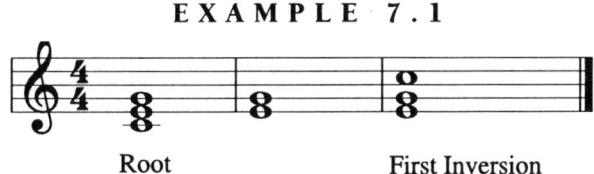

Root   First Inversion

The first chord is a "C" in root position. If we omit the bottom "C", but keep the "E" and the "G", we will need to continue up the scale until we find the next "C". We have taken the "C" off of the <u>bottom</u> of the chord and moved it up to the <u>top</u> of the chord. We have <u>inverted</u> the chord one time, thus the term **first inversion chord**.

This new right flag chord shape is illustrated in Example 7.2.

EXAMPLE 7.2
C Chord - 1st inversion

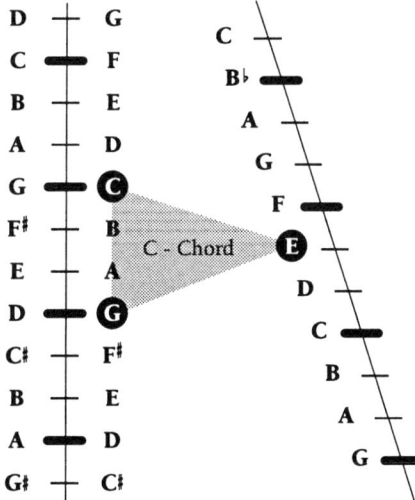

Remember that in <u>root position chords</u>, the name of the chord was the <u>first</u> note you played. Now that we have <u>inverted</u> it, the name of the chord is the <u>last</u> note you play. Because it is the last note, we will discuss first inversions based on that last note. So, this first example ends on a marked course. First inversion chords that end on a marked course are <u>major chords</u>. Practice the chords you see in Examples 7.3 & 7.4.

EXAMPLE 7.3
First inversion chords

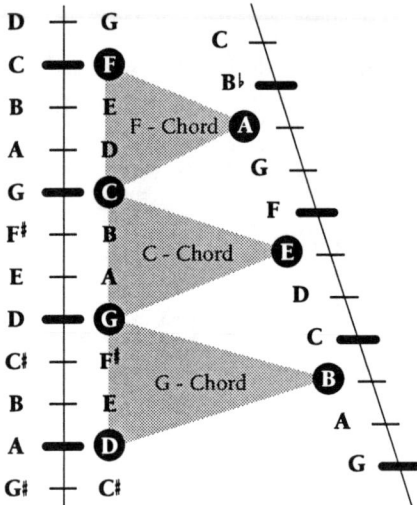

EXAMPLE 7.4
First inversion chords

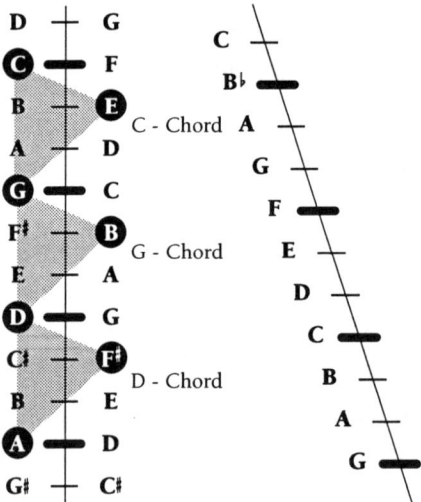

Let's look at first inversion chords that end one above a marked course. These chords are minor chords. Practice these first inversions illustrated in Examples 7.5 & 7.6.

EXAMPLE 7.5
First inversions - one above a marked course

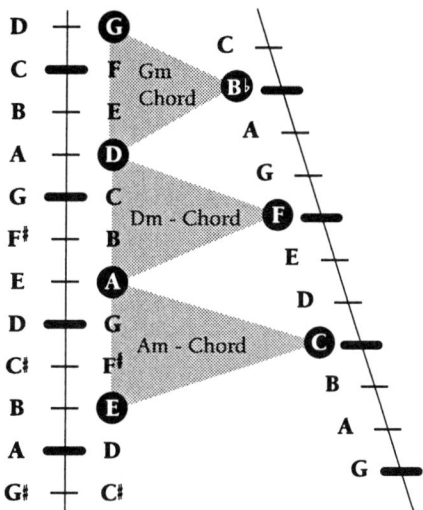

EXAMPLE 7.6
First inversions - one above a marked course

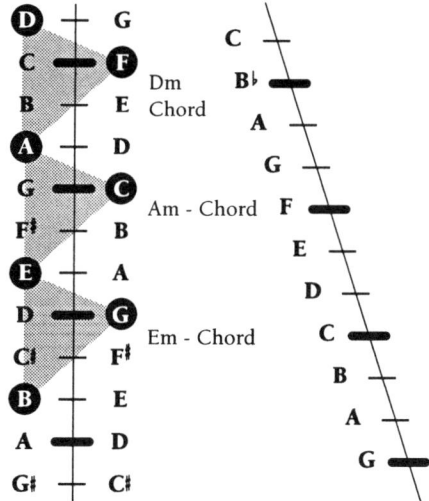

First inversion chords that end one below a marked course are also minor chords. Practice these chords illustrated in Example 7.7 & 7.8.

EXAMPLE 7.7
First inversions - one below a marked course

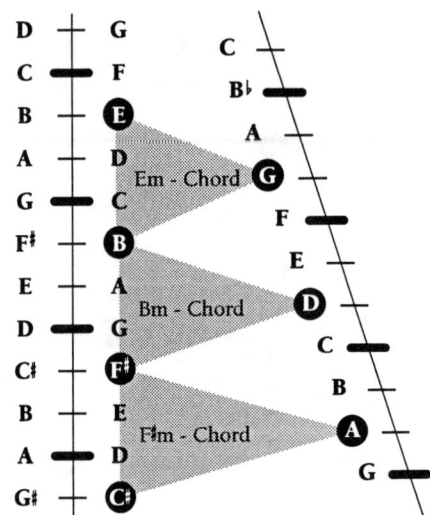

EXAMPLE 7.8
First inversions - one below a marked course

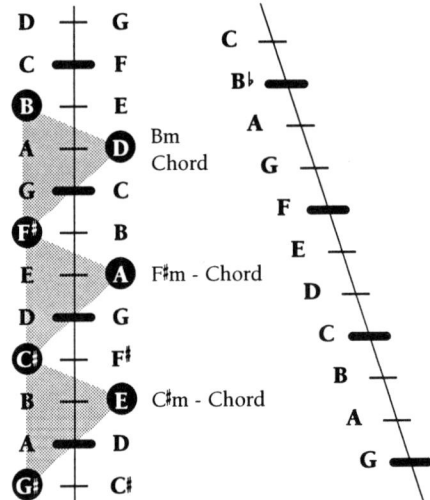

What happens when we flip these chords to left flag chords? Left flag first inversions that end on a marked course stay the same as right flag first inversions. They are still <u>major chords</u>. Practice these chords illustrated in Examples 7.9 & 7.10.

EXAMPLE 7.9
First inversions - marked course

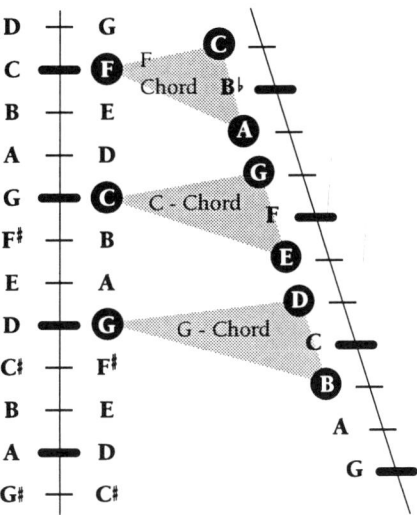

EXAMPLE 7.10
First inversions - marked course

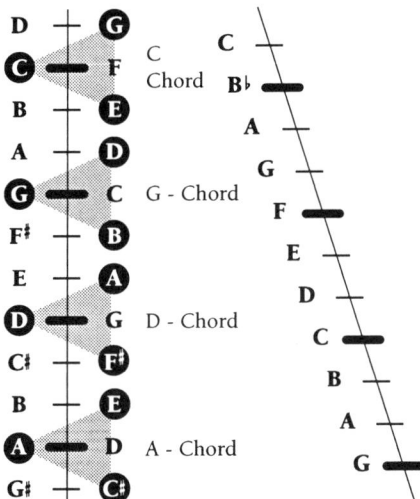

Left flag first inversions that end one above a marked course stay the same as their right flag counterparts. The right flags were minor chords, and the left flags are also **minor chords**. Practice these chords illustrated in Examples 7.11 & 7.12.

EXAMPLE 7.11
First inversions - one above a marked course

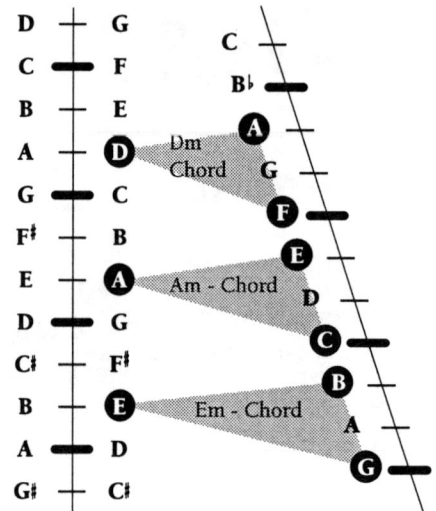

EXAMPLE 7.12
First inversions - one above a marked course

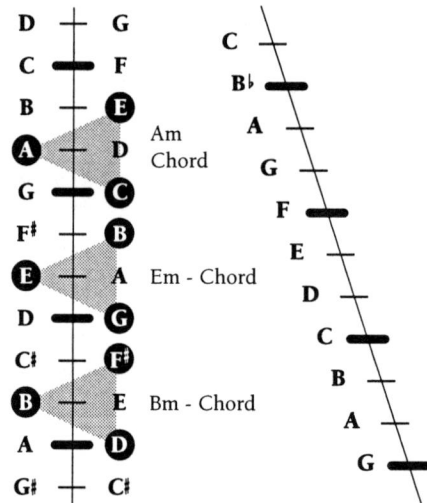

Left flag first inversions that end one below a marked course are not major or minor chords. They are **diminished chords**. This type of chord is rarely used in music played on the hammered dulcimer but you may want to practice the shape for different kinds of music that you may attempt later. These chords are shown in Examples 7.13 & 7.14.

EXAMPLE 7.13
Diminished Chords

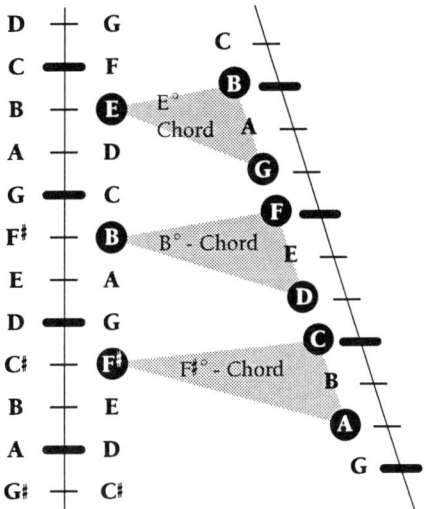

EXAMPLE 7.14
Diminished Chords

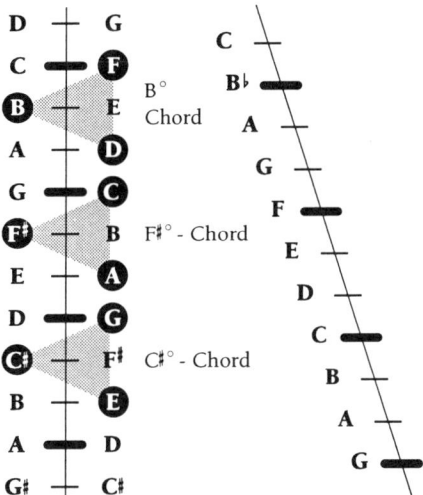

This lesson has covered a large amount of information in a very short space. Your mind may be reeling with right flags, left flags, majors, minors, roots and first inversions. We still have one important type of chord to deal with, the second inversion. In order to minimize confusion, it is probably best that you take time and review root position chords in lessons 1-3, and then take your time to thoroughly learn first inversions before you continue on with the next lesson. It will be equally intense.

Second Inversions

LESSON 8

In lesson 7 we used the example of a "C" root position chord being inverted one time on the staff. A **second inversion** takes the process one step further. In Example 8.1 you see a root position "C" chord that has been changed to a first inversion. If we omit the bottom note in the first inversion chord, the "E", and then move up on the staff until we find the next "E", we have inverted the chord a second time, and now we have our second inversion.

EXAMPLE 8.1

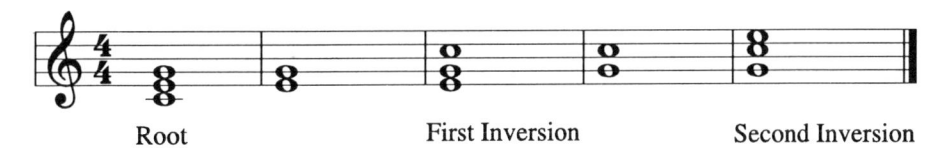

Root   First Inversion   Second Inversion

It's still a "C" chord, but now the "C" is in the <u>middle</u> instead of being on the bottom or the top of the chord. Like before, this will influence how we visualize the chord on the hammered dulcimer. Our first example has the name of the chord, or the middle note, on a marked course. See Examples 8.2 and 8.3 for right flag second inversion chords with the middle note on a marked course. These are <u>major chords</u>.

EXAMPLE 8.2
Second Inversions - marked course

C Chord: E, C, G
G - Chord: B, G, D
D - Chord: F#, D, A

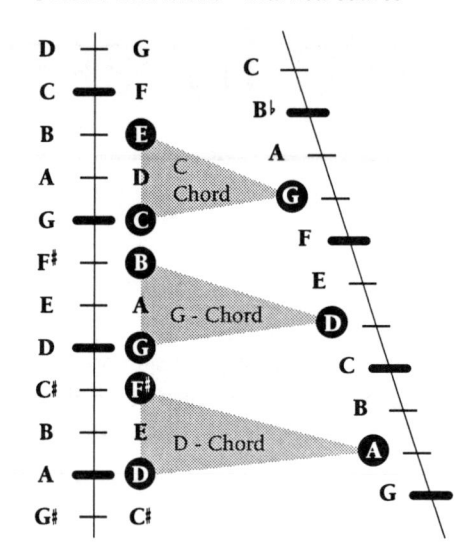

EXAMPLE 8.3
Second Inversions - marked course

G - Chord: B, G, D
D - Chord: F#, D, A
A - Chord: C#, A, E

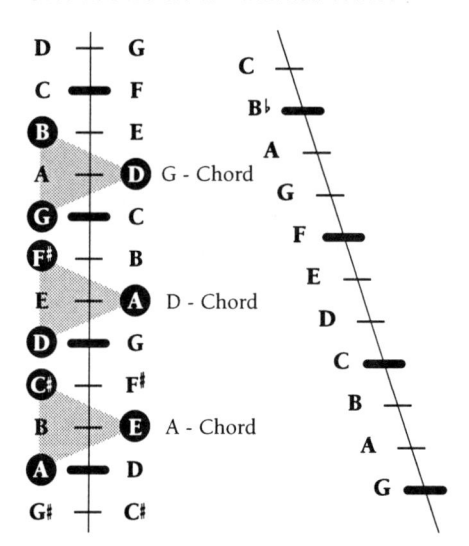

Right flag second inversions with the middle note one above a marked course are <u>minor chords</u>. See Examples 8.4 & 8.5 for this shape.

EXAMPLE 8.4
Second Inversions - one above a marked course

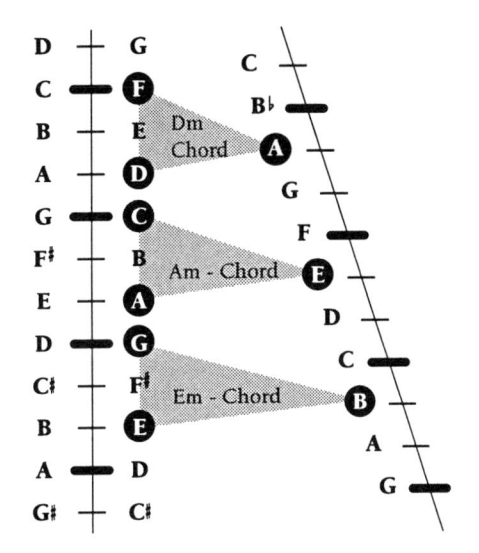

EXAMPLE 8.5
Second Inversions - one above a marked course

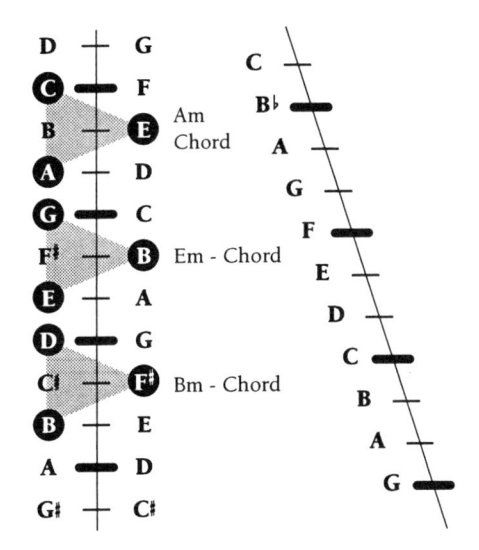

Right flag second inversions with the middle note one below a marked course are <u>diminished chords</u>. See Examples 8.6 &8.7 for these shapes.

EXAMPLE 8.6
Diminished Chords

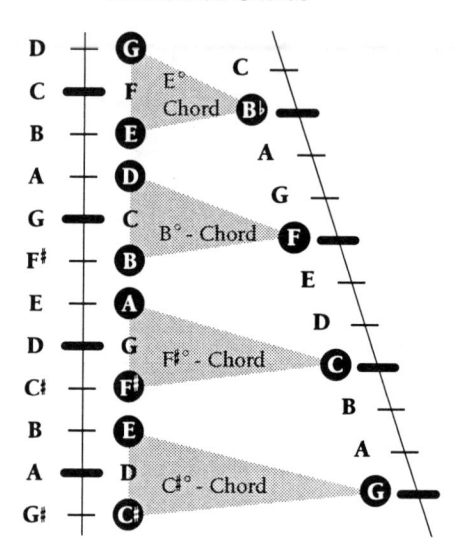

EXAMPLE 8.7
Diminished Chords

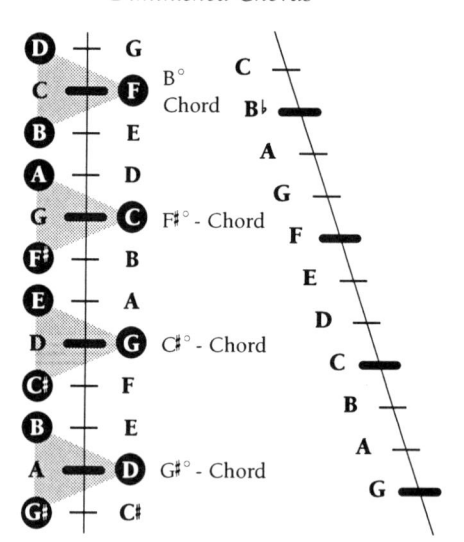

Once again, let's try to flip these chords to their left flag counterparts. Up until this point, every time we have flipped a chord we have left the first note and the last note in the same position and have changed the position of the middle note. Now the name of our chord is on that middle note. It doesn't really make a difference in the sounding of the chord. I just don't want you to become confused when that note changes position. Because of this, I will illustrate the left flag counterparts to the right flag second inversions below without much discussion. The first shape illustrated in Examples 8.8 & 8.9 remain major chords.

EXAMPLE 8.8

Second Inversions - major chords

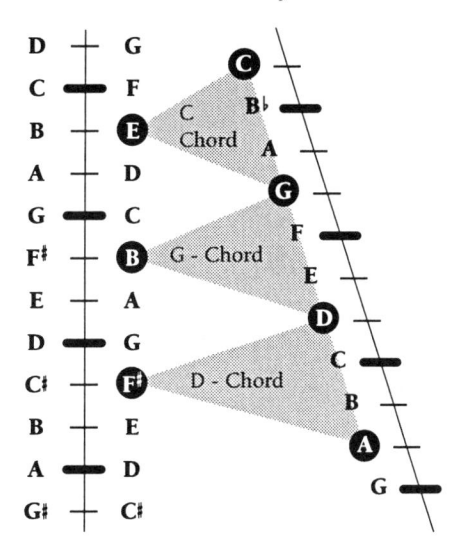

EXAMPLE 8.9

Second Inversions - major chords

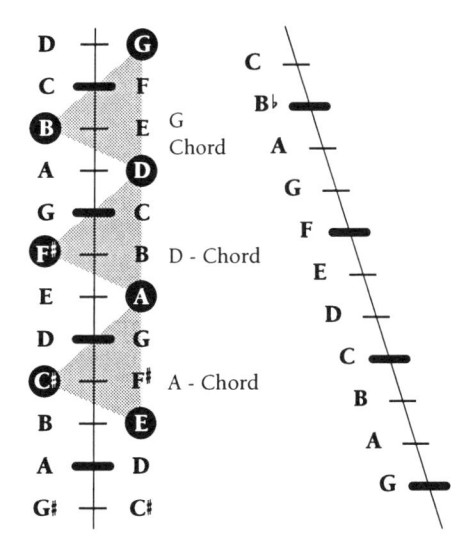

The second shape illustrated in Examples 8.10 & 8.11 remain <u>minor chords</u>.

EXAMPLE 8.10
Second Inversions - minor chords

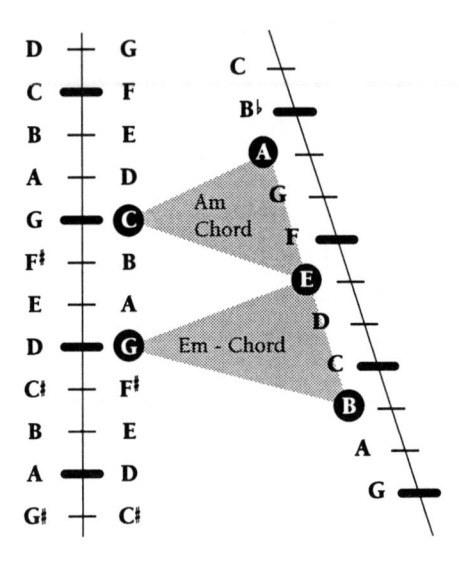

EXAMPLE 8.11
Second Inversions - minor chords

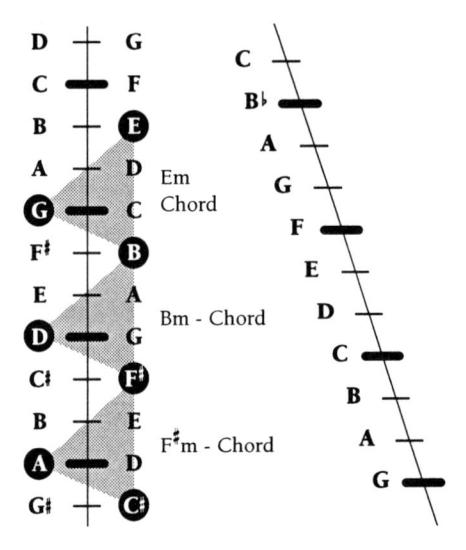

While the right flag version of this chord was diminished, the left flag version is a <u>major chord</u>. Practice this third shape illustrated in Examples 8.12 & 8.13.

EXAMPLE 8.12
Second Inversions - major chords

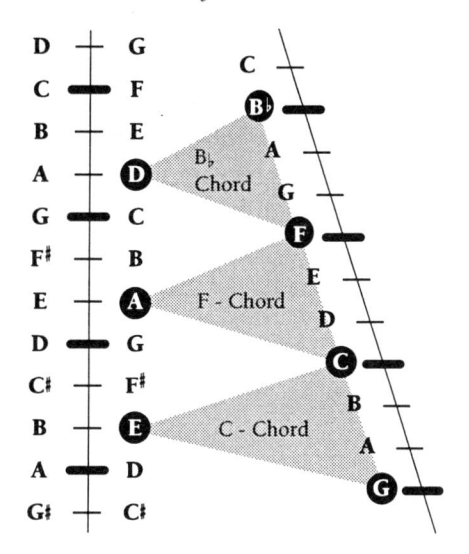

EXAMPLE 8.13
Second Inversions - major chords

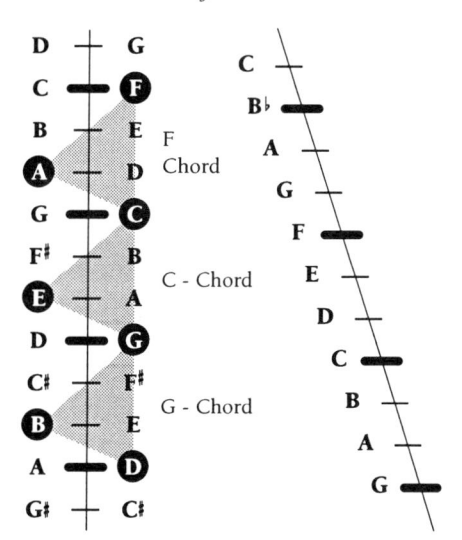

If you weren't overwhelmed at the end of lesson 7, you probably are now! It is likely that you will have to use first and second inversions over a long period of time before the rules governing them are internalized. At this stage, it is just important for you to realize that you have many chord options in both right flag and left positions. You now have the information necessary to at least locate the chord you are seeking. Some of these chords illustrated are rarely used. You, however, will eventually memorize those chords that are more commonly used on your instrument, and be able to locate them quickly and accurately, and play them smoothly.

REVIEW LESSONS 7-8

1. **First Inversion Chords**
    a. Right Flags that end on a marked course are <u>major chords</u>.
    b. Right Flags that end one above a marked course are <u>minor chords</u>.
    c. Right Flags that end one below a marked course are <u>minor chords</u>.
    d. Left Flags that end on a marked course are <u>major chords</u>.
    e. Left Flags that end one above a marked course are <u>minor chords</u>.
    f. Left Flags that end one below a marked course are <u>diminished</u>.

2. **Second Inversion Chords**
    a. Right Flags with the middle note on a marked course are <u>major chords</u>.
    b. When flipped to a left flag position this chord remains a <u>major chord</u>.
    c. Right Flags with the middle note one above a marked course are <u>minor chords</u>.
    d. When flipped to a left flag position this chord remains a <u>minor chord</u>.
    e. Right Flags with the middle note one below a marked course are <u>diminished</u>.
    f. When flipped to a left flag position this chord becomes a <u>major chord</u>.

A New Tune

LESSON 9

Now that we have the tools needed to locate chords, let's take a new tune and try to embellish the melody line. Figure 9.1 has a simple melody line written out with the accompaniment chords written above in "fake book" fashion.

EXAMPLE 9.1
Flow Gently Sweet Afton

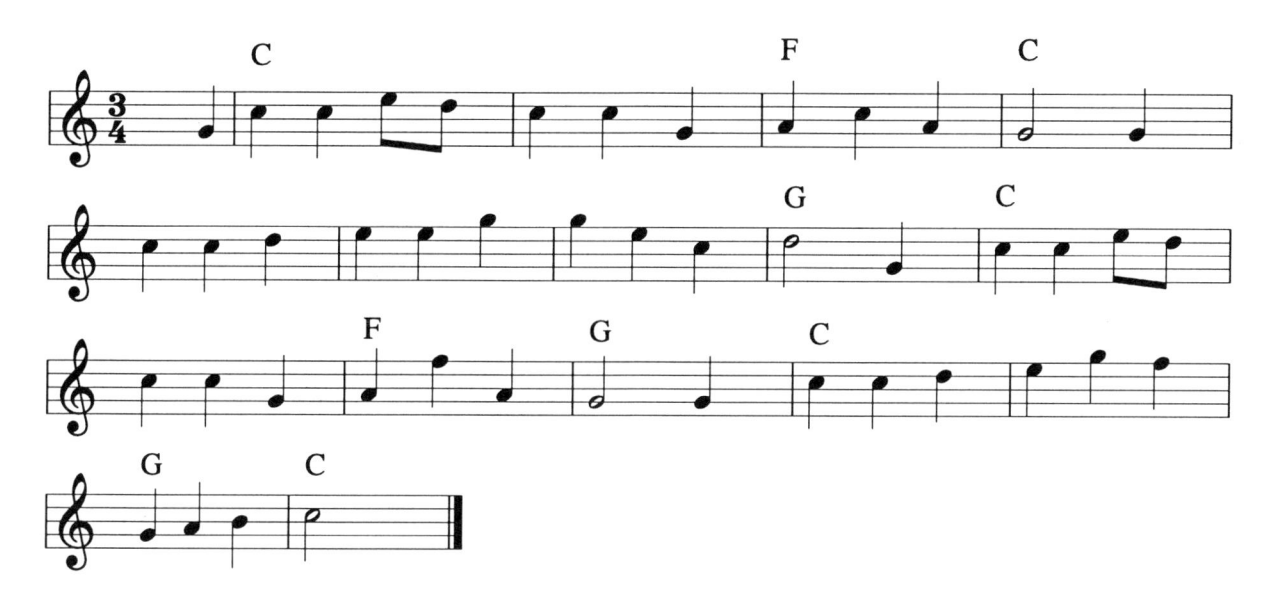

Let's try to discover the kinds of chords we will need if we roll a chord on the downbeat of each measure. We can see from the letter above the staff that measure 1 requires a "C" chord. What is the first note of measure 1? It is also a "C." We know that we will be rolling our chord up to the melody line so the last note we hit will be that "C." What kind of chord has the name of the chord on the top (the last note we hit)? A first inversion chord does. So we can roll a first inversion "C" chord on the first note of measure 1. (See Example 9.2)

ARRANGING FOR HAMMERED DULCIMER

EXAMPLE 9.2

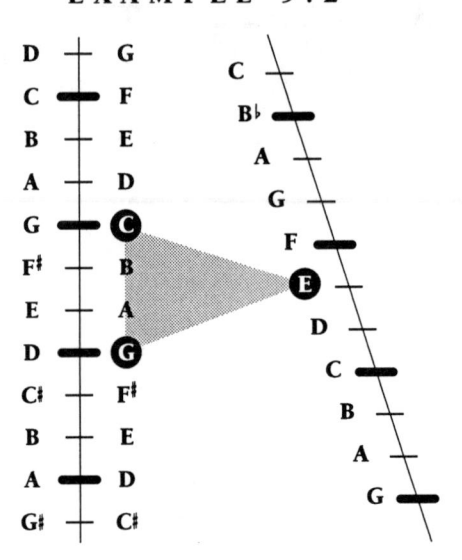

Measure 2 is exactly the same. It is still a "C" chord and it is also a "C" note, so once again, we can roll a "C" first inversion on the downbeat.

Measure 3 has changed chords. According to the letter indicated above the staff, we now need to find an "F" chord. We can see that the melody note on the downbeat is not an "F" so it must not be a first inversion chord. Let's experiment for a moment. Play a root position "F" chord. (Do you remember the shape from Lesson 1? See Example 9.3)

EXAMPLE 9.3

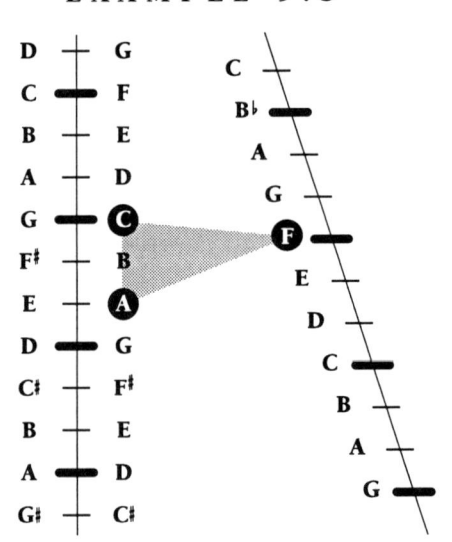

We can see that a root position "F" chord ends on a "C" note so that will not work either. Our only remaining option is an "F" second inversion. (See Example 9.4)

EXAMPLE 9.4

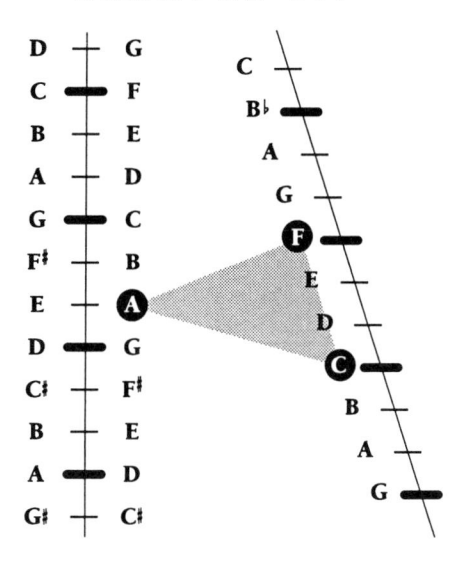

An "F" <u>second inversion</u> does end on an "A" note so that is our choice for measure 3.

The letter above measure 4 indicates that we have changed back to a "C" chord. We are not rolling up to a "C" note as in measure 1 so it can't be a first inversion. Now, let's try a root position chord (Example 9.5).

EXAMPLE 9.5

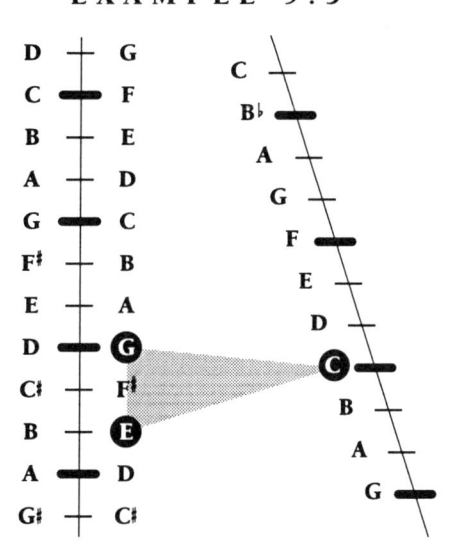

Yes, a <u>root position</u> "C" chord does roll up to a "G" note so that is the choice for measure 4.

Now you try to figure out the remaining chord choices for this song. There are several chords that repeat themselves over and over throughout the tune so much of the work is already done for you. The process of figuring out the chords is important, so I encourage you to stick with the melody written out in Example 9.1 and work your way through to the end. If you are getting frustrated, however,

Example 9.6 has the song re-written with the chords inserted. If you are having a hard time figuring out which chord you need, check the music, find the individual notes, and then identify the final chord shape.

EXAMPLE 9.6
Flow Gently Sweet Afton

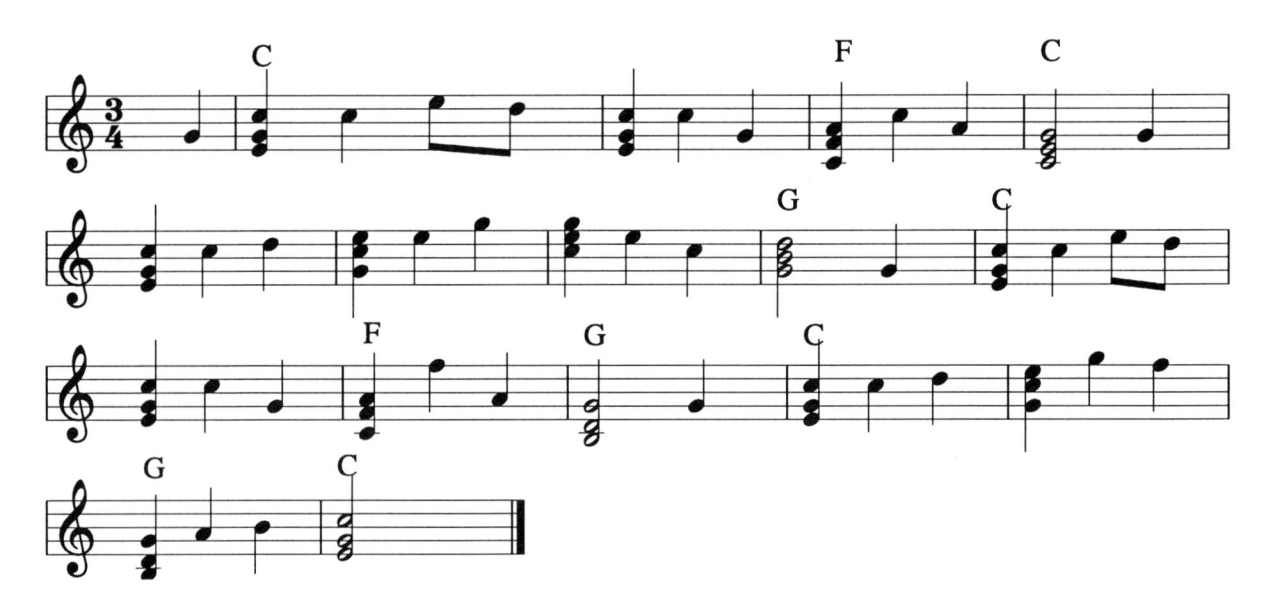

When looking at chords already written out on the staff (as in Example 9.6) there is another visual aid you can use. We already discovered that root position chords are easy to identify because they are found in a tight, even cluster of three notes (See Example 9.7).

EXAMPLE 9.7

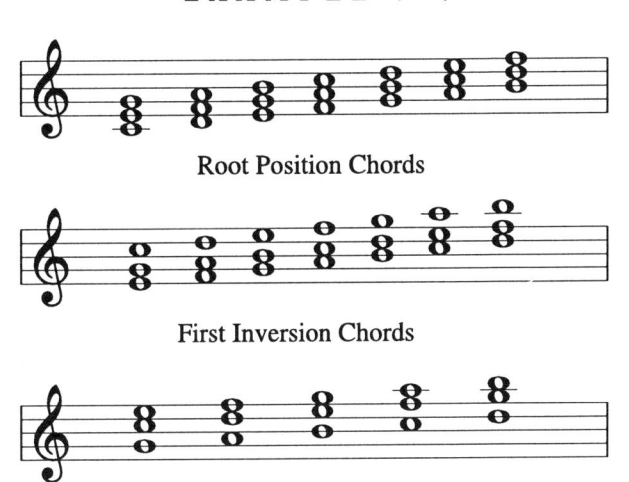

Root Position Chords

First Inversion Chords

Second Inversion Chords

First inversions always look like a cluster of two notes with the higher note further separated from them. (Example 9.7)

Second inversions always look like a cluster of two notes with the lower note further separated from them. (Example 9.7)

This is a simple method to quickly identify visually what kind of chord shape you might be using.

Now that you've walked through the process of finding triads to embellish a tune, try it on some of your own favorites.

Irish Jigs
LESSON 10

The triads (three note chords) that we have been working with so far add a beautiful and elegant touch to a slow song. But what about the faster tunes so commonly heard on the dulcimer today? Many of these tunes come from the Irish and Scottish traditions and were originally dance music, played on a fiddle, flute, pipes or whistle. Each has a unique rhythmic aspect that is necessary for the foot patterns used in dance. Let's begin with one of the most common: the Irish Jig. Jigs are in 6/8 time with an emphasis on beats 1 and 4. Usually jigs make use of dotted quarter notes, a quarter note and an eighth note (single jig), or groups of three eighth notes (double jig).

Try playing the jig written out in Example 10.1.

EXAMPLE 10.1
Tobin's Favorite

As you can see, it is a very nice tune just on its own. But suppose you wanted to add more to create a bit of an arrangement. These dance tunes move at a fairly quick pace, so you probably don't have time to roll a chord up to the melody line. You can add some intervals though, without affecting the flow of the music. Look at the chords written in above the staff of the music. Let's add some intervals under the melody line in the various places. (Like rolling chords, the general rule of thumb is to place harmony notes under the melody note because our ear hears the highest note most prominently and you don't want to lose the melody in a sea of other sounds).

Look at the first note in measure one. We can see that a "D" chord is being used. Find a "D" chord on your dulcimer. What three notes make up a "D" chord? That's right, "D", "F#", and "A". The note in the melody is a "D", so we have two other choices. Let's try adding an "A" underneath, so the measure looks like the one in Example 10.2.

EXAMPLE 10.2

Try the same thing with the first note in measure 2. The chord has changed to an "A". An "A" chord consists of an "A", a "C#", and an "E". The melody note is an "E" so choose either an "A" or a "C#" to play with it. I chose the C#. (The chord notated is actually an A7 chord. A seventh chord uses the three basic notes of the chord and adds another note a third higher, the note an interval of a seventh above the root. In this example, it uses the "A," the "C#," and the "E" found in an A major chord and adds the seventh note in the scale, the "G." If you don't want to concern yourself with the seventh chord, you can still use the basic major chord indicated.)

Try adding notes in other places throughout the song, always choosing a note that fits in the chord indicated above the staff. Remember that the first beat and the fourth beat tend to be emphasized in a jig, so you may want to add harmony in those places. You will soon see that you can overdo it if you're not careful. Don't add too much harmony. Experiment with the melody to see where the most important notes are that need to be emphasized.

Another option to add spice to your fast arrangements is with the use of **grace notes**. People who play bagpipes and small pipes are very comfortable with these quick, short notes added to the melody line. These cuts (as they are called) separate repeated notes, and emphasize accented notes. You will notice this type of ornamentation used by Celtic fiddlers, whistle players, harpers, etc. with each musician tailoring the technique to his or her instrument. On the hammered dulcimer, the easiest way to achieve this is to employ the **bounce**. If you hold your hammer high above the strings and then let it drop, the hammer will bounce multiple times before coming to a stop. You can use finger pressure to control the number of times the hammer bounces on the string—two, three, four or more—and then insert them in various spots. Try using both hammers to sustain the bounce for longer periods of time. This is noted on my music with three slashes through the stem of the note. Once you have practiced and mastered this technique, you can move the hammer from one string to another in the midst of a bounce to achieve the grace note. Now, go back to Example 10.1 and add your own notes to create an arrangement.

Example 10.3 illustrates the intervals and grace notes that I have chosen to add to this tune. Is yours similar?

EXAMPLE 10.3
Tobin's Favorite

Before you go on to work on your own tunes, you should be aware that there are different kinds of jigs. For example, slip jigs are just like a jig, but they are played in 9/8 time so you need three groups of three beats in each measure instead of two. The accents are on beats 1, 4, and 7. The rhythm and accents are just slightly different. Keep that in mind when you are arranging pieces other than the basic single jig or double jig.

HORNPIPES

LESSON 11

Hornpipes are written in 4/4 time and are played slower than jigs. Hornpipes have a "bouncy" feel to them because the notes are most often paired in groups of one dotted eighth note tied to a sixteenth note—the emphasis is on the first note of each pairing. Be forewarned that in some music, you will find hornpipe tunes written with straight eighth notes, and it is assumed that you, the player, understand that the "bouncy" feeling is to be added.

Triplets are also quite common in hornpipes. Notice in these few measures taken from the hornpipe "Harvest Home" a straightforward approach to the melody. (Example 11.1)

EXAMPLE 11.1
Harvest Home

The most common version heard, however, is seen in Example 11.2. See how triplets changed the interest level.

EXAMPLE 11.2
Harvest Home

Example 11.3 is a hornpipe for you to try. The melody is written out for you with the chords above the staff just as before. Use your knowledge of chord theory, just as you did with the jigs, to find an arrangement to your liking.

EXAMPLE 11.3
The Friendly Visit

After you have worked the tune yourself, you can compare it with my choices in Example 11.4.

EXAMPLE 11.4

Reels

LESSON 12

Reels, like hornpipes, are written in 4/4 time but the accent is usually on the first note of a four-note group (beats 1 and 3). Reels are played very fast (some would say that we hammered dulcimists play them too fast!). These are fun to just fly on, though, so I find that I add very little in the way of embellishment. Example 12.1 is the melody for you to try yourself, and Example 12.2 shows you the choices I have made for the tune.

EXAMPLE 12.1
The Green Fields of America

EXAMPLE 12.2
The Green Fields of America

Although jigs, reels and hornpipes are the most common Celtic styles played on the hammered dulcimer there are others for you to try as well. Polkas, marches, waltzes, and the Scottish strathspey, are just a few that you may want to research and give a try. The rhythm patterns are just slightly different, but the techniques you have learned using basic chord theory will apply to other styles as well. Just pay attention to the beats that are accented for each particular style and build chordal support underneath the melody note in those places.

Review
Lessons 10-12

1. Fast tunes require that we use fewer notes to embellish a tune.

2. On accented beats, we usually pick one note from the chord that is underneath the melody note, both to be played simultaneously.

3. Jigs are written in 6/8 time with the accents on beat one and four.

4. Slip jigs are in 9/8 time with three groupings of three notes rather than two groupings.

5. Use the bounce technique for adding grace notes.

6. Hornpipes are written in 4/4 time and have a "bouncy" feel to them because of the dotted-eighth-note/sixteenth-note pairings, with each group of two being accented.

7. Triplets are often added to hornpipe tunes.

8. Reels are played fast with accents on beats one and three.

MORE FILLS
LESSON 13

Let's return now to some of the slower tunes that give us more room to add ornamentation. You may have already discovered that while rolled chords add a lot to a naked melody line, sometimes they don't add enough. Even though the hammered dulcimer is noted for its ability to sustain notes (sometimes for too long a period of time), the note that has been struck is still in the process of dying immediately. It is not like a fiddle or a flute that can continue to produce a strong note for the full length of a whole note. It is necessary, then, to "fill" up some of the empty spaces. It's important to realize that these fill notes must be secondary, deferring to the importance of the melody line. You don't want your melody line to be lost in a barrage of extra notes. That defeats the purpose. Everything you do to arrange a tune should add to, embellish and support the melody line. Don't overwhelm the melody, and don't allow too many notes to ring, muddying up the sound. We can accomplish this by being careful not to add too many fills, and to hit them more lightly than notes in the melody line.

Arpeggio is a fancy word that describes the act of playing a broken chord. We can take the chords we've already learned and break them up to fill the empty spots. In Example 13.1 we have a simple melody line.

EXAMPLE 13.1
Amazing Grace

In Example 13.2 we have added some rolled chords.

EXAMPLE 13.2
Amazing Grace

In Example 13.3 we have added some broken chords to fill out the empty spots.

EXAMPLE 13.3
Amazing Grace

There are other ways to fill up empty spaces. Try running a simple **scale** from one melody note to the other. I often run a scale when moving from verse to chorus or vice versa (See Example 13.4).

EXAMPLE 13.4
Joy to the World

A simple way to fill up extra space is to **double** your hammers on several notes in a row. (Examples 13.5 & 13.6)

EXAMPLE 13.5
Old Joe Clark

EXAMPLE 13.6
Old Joe Clark

If you speed up the doubling technique and play them very fast, you create a **tremolo** effect that mimics the sound associated with a mandolin.

Emphasize an important note by walking around it. (Examples 13.7 & 13.8)

EXAMPLE 13.7
Banks of the Ohio

EXAMPLE 13.8
Banks of the Ohio

Experiment with other ways to fill the gaps around a melody line.

COUNTER MELODIES
LESSON 14

As you can see from the last chapter, you don't always have to use chords to embellish a tune. You may want to try creating a **counter melody**. A counter melody is a completely different melody line that sounds good with the established melody line. The most common counter melody uses **parallel motion**, meaning that the two melodies both go up in pitch in the same places, and go down in pitch in the same places. This is usually accomplished by adding the counter melody a third down from the original melody. (See Example 14.1. I've added a counter melody to lines 1 and 3—you try to add to lines 2 and 4.)

EXAMPLE 14.1
Ode to Joy

A counter melody that uses **contrary motion** travels in the opposite direction of the established melody line. When the melody line goes up, the counter melody goes down, and so on. (See Examples 14.2 & 14.3)

EXAMPLE 14.2
Wildwood Flower

EXAMPLE 14.3
Wildwood Flower

Another technique is to **echo** the melody line. (See Example 14.4)

EXAMPLE 14.4
Silent Night

It is best if each of these methods is used sparingly, sometimes for just a measure or two. Just as we found that too many chords can overwhelm a melody line, too many fills and counter melodies can do the same thing. One exception to this is to create a completely new melody line. This is accomplished by taking the same chord progression used for the original melody line and make up a new stand-alone melody. You can play the melodies one after the other, or arrange them so you play them both at the same time. It is believed that the famous 17th century harper Turlough O'Carolan did this with his song "Beauty in Tears" which fits beautifully with the Welsh folk tune "Ash Grove". In Example 14.5 I've written a counter melody to fit with the simple tune "The Root Waltz" used in Lesson 6. Go back to Lesson 6 and play example 6.1. Now play Example 14.5.

EXAMPLE 14.5

The Root Waltz Counter Melody

Play one after another and see how they are two different tunes. In Example 14.6, I've written them both together so you can hear how one embellishes the other.

EXAMPLE 14.6

The Root Waltz Counter Melody

Find a simple tune and you give it a try.

USING YOUR BASS BRIDGE
LESSON 15

For some reason we hammered dulcimer players often find ourselves hovering around the middle of the treble bridge. Don't be afraid of using that bass bridge! I'm sure that some of our reluctance to use those strings comes from the fact that we know that those notes will ring even longer. Because of this, I recommend that you hit them lightly and sparingly—but do use them. The occasional use of **bass notes** will lend to a melody.

Open chords are a good idea when using low tones, so that the notes don't sound muddy. For a nice, open, sound trying using the tonic, the fifth and the octave note. (See Example 15.1)

EXAMPLE 15.1

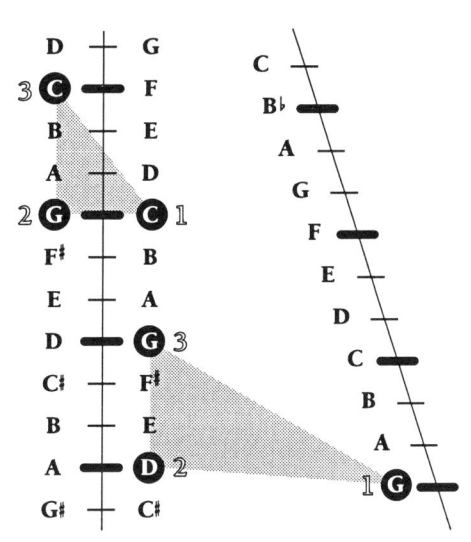

Another nice addition is to add a **walking bass line**. This is when you literally walk notes straight up or down your bass bridge. (See Example 15.2)

EXAMPLE 15.2
Early One Morning

FOUR-NOTE CHORDS

LESSON 16

When we began our discussion about chords we focused mainly on triads, those chords having three notes in them. Later, we suggested that you choose just two notes from a triad for faster tunes. You can also add notes to a triad to make the chord thicker and richer. Let's look at our basic right flag root position "C" chord. The chord ends with a "G" note. If we take that note and add the same one on the bottom we have created a **four-note chord**. See Example 16.1 for the chord shape. It forms a lop-sided **box** shape.

EXAMPLE 16.1

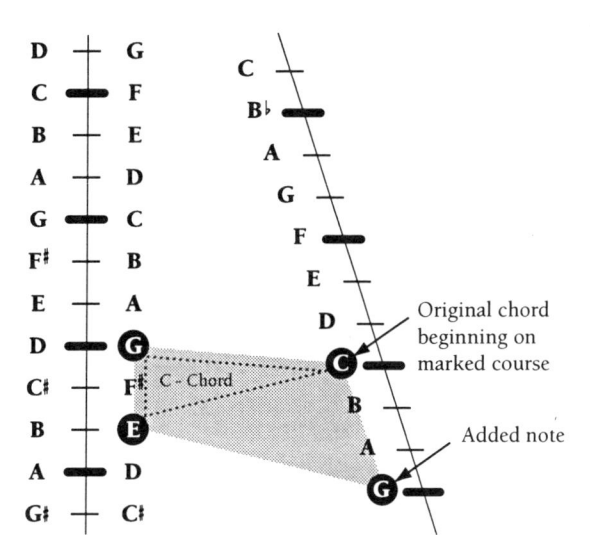

Try moving this chord around on your dulcimer and notice that it works with chords in the other starting positions: one above a marked course and one below a marked course. (See Example 16.2)

EXAMPLE 16.2

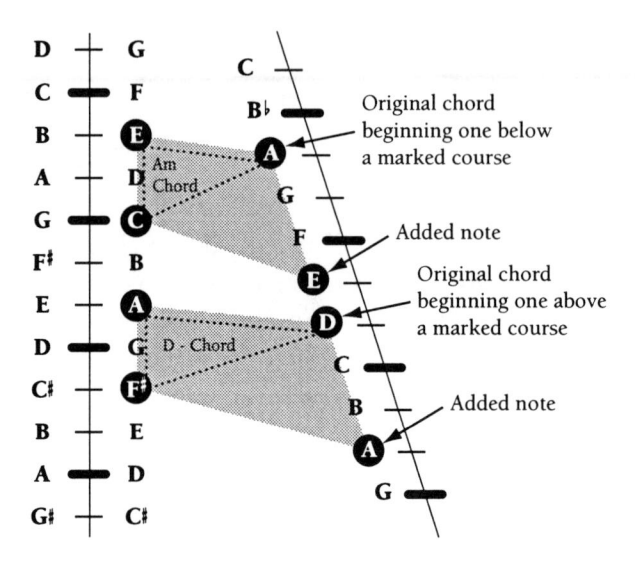

If you look closely at this chord you will see that the bottom part is actually a left flag chord. Like a jigsaw puzzle, the pieces fit together to form one four-note chord. (See Example 16.3)

EXAMPLE 16.3

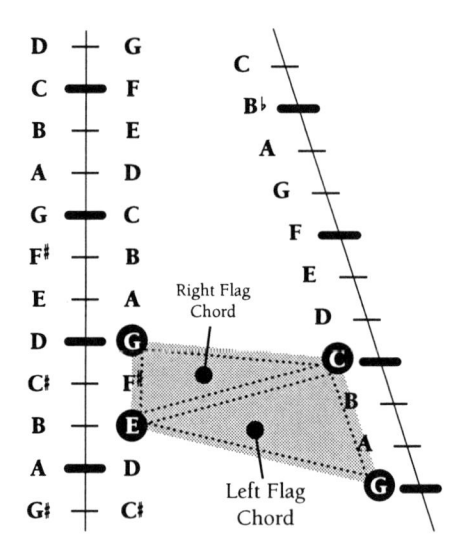

Try adding a note on the bottom of first inversions and second inversions, then note how they, too, can be taken apart to form both right and left flag chords. Notice, also, how the box changes shape slightly (Examples 16.4 & 16.5)

EXAMPLE 16.4

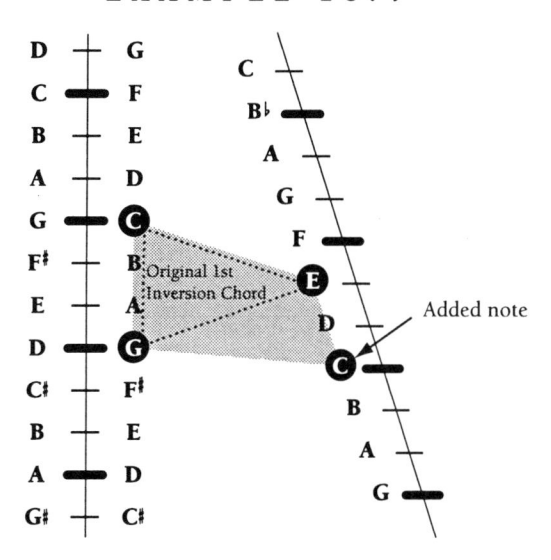

EXAMPLE 16.5

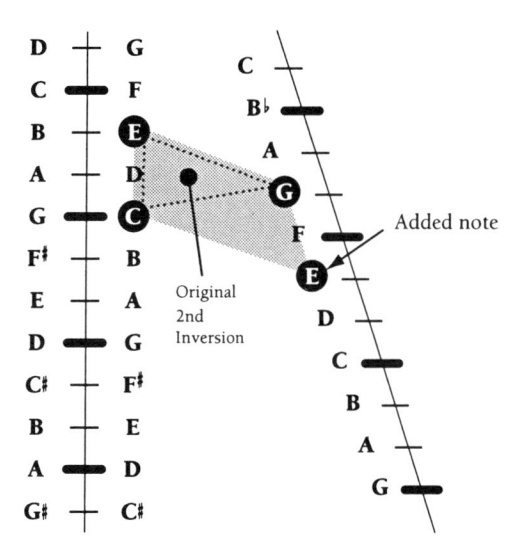

Let's take a right flag root position chord that begins one above a marked course. If you add a note on the top of the chord, it forms a **diamond** shape. (See Example 16.6)

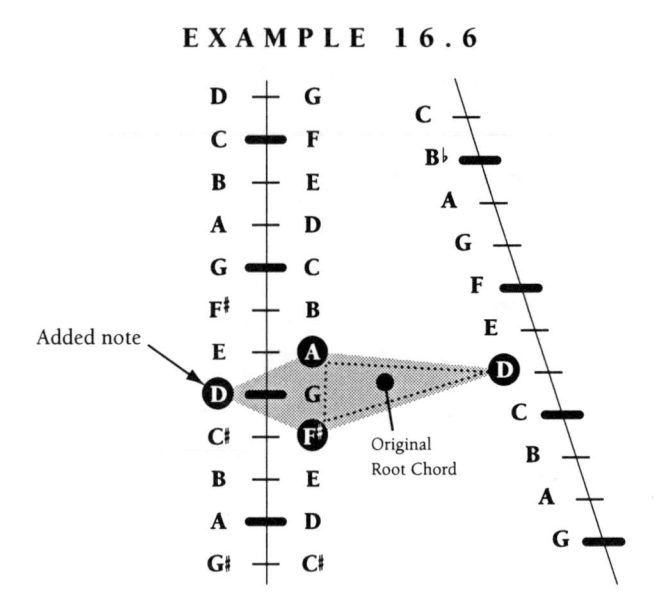

EXAMPLE 16.6

If we tried to form a diamond chord using a right flag root position chord that begins on a marked course, we would not be successful. That's because the note on the other side of the treble bridge is not a C natural, but a C sharp. Experiment with adding a note on the top of first and second inversions (see Example 16.7).

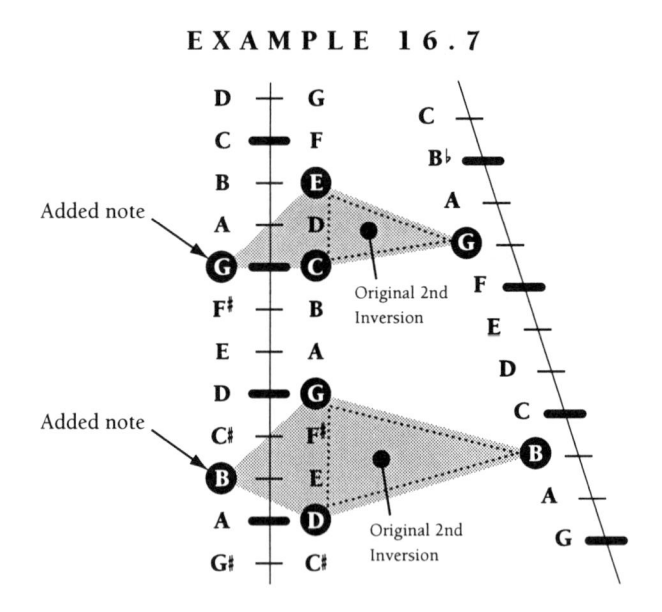

EXAMPLE 16.7

Like the box shapes, these four-note chords can also be broken down into a right flag and left flag shape. (Example 16.8)

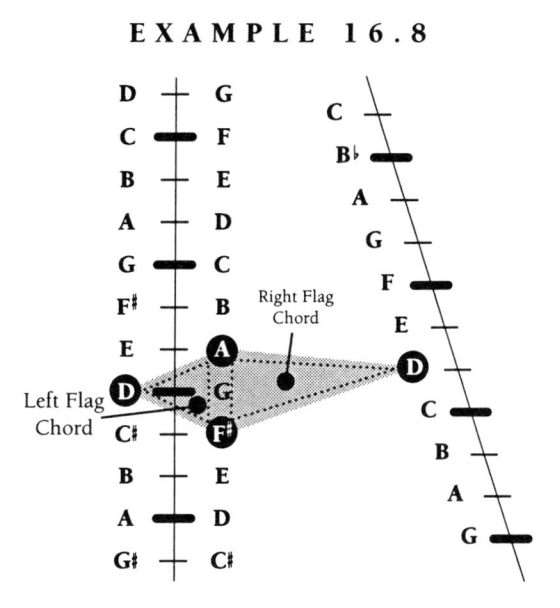

EXAMPLE 16.8

As you become more familiar with these interlocking pieces, you will begin to see that your dulcimer is very much like a huge jigsaw puzzle with one chord building on another. You'll also discover that you don't need to stop at four-note chords. Just keep adding notes above or underneath the basic chord.

Try changing the three note chords we used earlier in "Amazing Grace" to four note chords (Example 16.9).

EXAMPLE 16.9
Amazing Grace

80

CHORD EXPERIMENTATION
LESSON 17

So far, we have spent a lot of time learning basic major and minor chords available to you on your instrument. There are many other chords at your disposal that we have not even touched upon. Diminished and augmented chords and the like are not typically used in traditional styles of music commonly played on the hammered dulcimer. There is no reason why you can't play other types of music, though, and so I encourage you to experiment with new chords. It is not necessary for you to understand all of the chord theory that goes along with these unusual chords. Use your ear and try things that sound good to you. Even changing the normally expected major chords to minor chords can enhance and change the tone of a common melody. Look at the lead line to "Simple Gifts" in Example 17.1. Play it as it is written.

EXAMPLE 17.1
Simple Gifts

Now, let's add some typical chords to the melody line. Play this version in Example 17.2.

EXAMPLE 17.2
Simple Gifts

Now, let's experiment with creating some new chord sounds (Example 17.3) Try this version now.

EXAMPLE 17.3
Simple Gifts

See what you can do to chords by just altering them slightly. You may not want to do this all the time, but it keeps us from getting in a rut of playing all of our tunes exactly the same.

Conclusion: Follow the Rules/Break the Rules/Make new Rules

LESSON 18

There are still some basic rules of music that we can employ to add to the arrangements we create.

* We can pay attention to the dynamics of our song. Where should we play loud, and where should we play soft? Are there places that we should gradually build in volume or places to grow softer?
* What is the emotion that your song should evoke? How can you accomplish that? Should you add a staccato section to a march to give it a military feel, or should you play that dreamy air smoothly and slowly?
* Move the melody up or down an octave.
* Change keys in the middle of the tune.

It's time to stop playing tunes and start making music. Play with feeling. Use the notes to communicate something. You've put many hours into learning your instrument and mastering technique, now put your heart into it.

You've learned plenty of musical rules over the years, and we've added some more throughout this book that pertain just to your instrument. Follow those rules diligently until you know them backwards and forwards—then start breaking them everywhere you can!

* So you have a standard tune written in 3/4 time? Change it to 4/4!
* Take a reel and play it like a hornpipe.
* Take a melody that is written in a major key and add minor chords instead.
* Take a familiar melody line and write a different ending to it.

Any rule that you can think of, try to find a way to break it. You'd be surprised how creative you can be. Make some new rules, too. Who says you have to hammer your instrument?

* Have you tried plucking the strings instead?
* How about using a pick to strum it like an autoharp?
* Who says you have to hit the strings only? Have you tried hammering on the wood, or on the bridges to see what different rhythm percussion sounds you can get?

* Have you seen the dulcimers with dampers on them? Don't have dampers? Lay a light cloth over part of your strings and try playing now.
* Do you have wooden hammers? Have you tried the aluminum ones?
* Have you tried adding leather, or cloth, or rubber bands, or whatever to your hammers?

Go out and make some new rules!

The point is, don't stop the creative process here. This book was only meant to get you started. You take it from here. It's time to take your favorite tunes and make them your own.

In Example 18.1 you will again find a "bare-bones" tune for you to arrange. After you try your hand at it, try my version, Example 18.2, which includes many of the techniques discussed in this book. Please try your own arrangement first, to see what you can come up with, and then compare the two. I would wager that you will see a remarkable difference. That is the point of arranging music. Arrange it so it is satisfying to your ear.

Hopefully this is just the beginning for you. Use these basic techniques to get you started, then see where your own creativity leads you. But most important: Have fun! (And happy hammering!)

EXAMPLE 18.1
The Foggy Dew

EXAMPLE 18.2
The Foggy Dew